a journey across the Arabian Peninsula

ABCs of Arabia

رحلة عبر شبه الجزيرة العربية

المعلومات الأساسية عن شبه الجزيرة العربية

Alison Hong Nguyen Lihalakha

أليسون هونغ نجوين ليهالاخا

KAHANA PRESS

Illustrated by Justine Braguy

الرسومات التوضيحية: جوستين براغي

Translated by Khaoula Mahouachi

ترجمة: خولة محواشي

Special thanks to Stephanie Ford, Bobbi Waldner and Karien Wilson

شكر خاص لستيفاني فورد، وبوبي والدنر، وكارين ويلسون

For the students of Dhahran Hills Elementary School

لطلاب مدرسة تلال الظهران الابتدائية

A is for Ahlan wa Sahlan أهلًا وسهلًا

Ahlan wa Sahlan (Welcome) to the Arabian Peninsula, home to some of the world's most significant cultural and religious sites, including the birthplace of Islam. This is a region characterized by its arid climate, vast desert landscapes, and rich cultural history. Let's explore!

أهلًا وسهلًا بكم في شبه الجزيرة العربية، التي تُعَد موطنًا لبعض أهم المواقع الثقافية والدينية في العالم، وهي المكان الذي وُلد فيه الإسلام. تتميَّز هذه المنطقة بمناخها الجاف ومناظرها الصحراوية الشاسعة، وتاريخها الثقافي الغني. هيا بنا نستكشفها!

B is for Bedouin   بدو

The Bedouin people are a group of nomadic Arab tribes traditionally living in the desert regions of the Middle East and North Africa.

البدو مجموعة من القبائل العربية الرُحَّل، يعيشون حياة تقليدية في المناطق الصحراوية في الشرق الأوسط وشمال أفريقيا.

C is for camel إبل

Camels have played a crucial role in the Arabian Peninsula for thousands of years, earning them the nickname "ships of the desert" due to their ability to travel long distances over barren terrain with little sustenance. They have served as a means of transportation, a source of food, and even in sports and beauty contests. Here, a group of camels, referred to as a caravan, is traveling through the desert.

لعبت الإبل دورًا مهمًا في شبه الجزيرة العربية منذ آلاف السنين، مما أكسبها لقب "سفن الصحراء"، لما تتمتّع به من قدرات في تحمُّل مشاق السفر لمسافات طويلة سيرًا على الأراضي القاحلة بقليل من المؤونة. خدمتِ الإبلُ الإنسانَ بوصفها وسيلة نقل، ومصدر غذاء له، حتى إنَّها تشارك اليوم في المسابقات الرياضية والجمالية. تظهر هنا مجموعة من الإبل، التي يُشار إليها باسم القافلة، وهي تسافر عبر الصحراء.

D is for dune bashing كثبان رملية

Much of the Arabian Peninsula is hot dry desert. One of the most popular activities is dune bashing. This involves driving a four-wheel-drive vehicle over the sand dunes at high speeds, which can be both exhilarating and challenging!

تغطي الصحراء الحارة والجافة جزءًا كبيرًا من شبه الجزيرة العربية، وتُعَد القيادة على الكثبان الرملية من أكثر الأنشطة شعبية فيها، إذ تتضمن قيادة سيارات ذات دفع رباعي فوق الكثبان الرملية بسرعات عالية، والتي يمكن أن تكون مليئة بالإثارة والتحديات!

E is for Empty Quarter ربع خالي

The Empty Quarter, officially known as Rub' al-Khali, is the largest sand desert in the world covering an area of approximately 250,000 square miles. It is almost as big as Texas and bigger than France. Located in the southern part of the Arabian Peninsula, it spans across Saudi Arabia, Oman, the United Arab Emirates, and Yemen.

صحراء "الربع الخالي" أكبر صحراء رملية في العالم، إذ إنها تغطي مساحة ٢٥٠ ألف ميل مربع تقريبًا، أي تقريبًا بحجم ولاية تكساس، وأكبر من مساحة فرنسا. تقع في الجزء الجنوبي من شبه الجزيرة العربية، وتمتد وصولًا إلى المملكة العربية السعودية، وسلطنة عمان، والإمارات العربية المتحدة، واليمن.

F is for falconry   الصقارة

Falconry is an ancient and culturally significant practice where trained falcons are used to hunt small animals like desert hares. It embodies a rich historical heritage and has evolved into a sport and a means of conservation, with falconry competitions and efforts to protect endangered bird species.

الصقارة ممارسة قديمة وذات أهمية ثقافية، تُستخدَم فيها الصقور المدربة لاصطياد الحيوانات الصغيرة مثل الأرانب البرية. تجسد الصقارة تراثاً تاريخياً غنياً، وقد تطورت لتصبح رياضة ووسيلة للحفاظ على البيئة، بفضل مسابقات الصقارة والجهود المبذولة لحماية أنواع الطيور المهددة بالانقراض.

F is also for fox   ثعلب

The Arabian red fox is a small carnivorous mammal found in the Arabian Peninsula and adjacent regions. It is primarily nocturnal and feeds on a variety of small animals, including rodents, insects, and reptiles.

الثعلب العربي الأحمر حيوان صغير لاحم ينتمي إلى فصيلة الثدييات، يعيش في شبه الجزيرة العربية والمناطق المجاورة، وهو حيوان ينشط ليلاً على نحوٍ رئيس، ويقتات على مجموعة متنوعة من الحيوانات الصغيرة مثل القوارض والحشرات والزواحف.

G is for gold ذهب

Gold mining in Arabia dates back 5,000 years. The Mahd Ad-Dhahab (Cradle of Gold) mine has been in operation for over 2,000 years. The gold produced in Saudi Arabia is used for jewelry making, investment, and industrial applications. Gold is a highly valued gift in courtship and marriage. The gold souk (market) is a popular place to buy jewelry and coins.

يعود تاريخ تعدين الذهب في شبه الجزيرة العربية إلى ٥،٠٠٠ سنة. المنجم المعروف باسم "مهد الذهب" في الخدمة منذ أكثر من ٢،٠٠٠ سنة. يُستخدَم الذهب المنتج في المملكة العربية السعودية في صناعة المجوهرات والاستثمار والتطبيقات الصناعية، ويُعَد الذهب هدية قيِّمة في مناسبات الخطوبة والزواج. سوق الذهب مكان شهير لشراء المجوهرات والعملات المعدنية.

H is for Hudhud   هدهد

The hudhud (hoopoe bird in English) is found in Europe, Asia, and Africa, and has a distinctive curved beak with a striking crest of feathers on its head. It is considered a symbol of good luck and protection in many cultures and is mentioned in several ancient texts, including the Bible and the Quran.

يعيش طائر الهدهد في أوروبا وآسيا وأفريقيا، ولديه منقار منحنٍ مميز وعُرف مذهل من الريش على رأسه. يُعَد الهدهد رمزًا للحظ السعيد والحماية في العديد من الثقافات، وقد ورد ذكره في العديد من النصوص القديمة، بما في ذلك الكتاب المقدس والقرآن.

I is for Ithra   إثراء

Ithra, or the King Abdulaziz Center for World Culture, is a cultural center located in Dhahran, Saudi Arabia. The center is a hub for knowledge, creativity, and innovation, featuring a library, museum, theater, and exhibition halls.

"مركز إثراء"، أو "مركز الملك عبد العزيز الثقافي العالمي"، مركز ثقافي يقع في مدينة الظهران بالمملكة العربية السعودية، ويُعَد مجمعًا للمعرفة والإبداع والابتكار، ويضم مكتبة ومتحفًا ومسرحًا وقاعات عرض.

J is for jebels جبل

Jebels are hills or small mountains, typically characterized by rugged terrain, steep slopes, and rocky surfaces, forming a distinctive appearance and providing a habitat for plants and animals.

Jebel Fihrayn, commonly known as the Edge of the World, is a 300-meter-tall (or 984 feet) rock formation northwest of Riyadh—almost as tall as the Eiffel Tower. It contains fossils and is the result of tectonic movement of the Arabian Plate.

الجبال مرتفعات أرضية تتميز عادةً بتضاريس وعرة ومنحدرات شديدة وسطوح صخرية، تشكِّل مظهرًا مميزًا، وتوفر موطنًا للنباتات والحيوانات.

جبل "فهرين"، المعروف باسم "حافة العالم"، تشكيل صخري يقع شمال غرب مدينة الرياض، ويبلغ ارتفاعه ٣٠٠ متر (أو ٩٨٤ قدمًا)، أي بارتفاع "برج إيفل" تقريبًا. وقد تكوَّنَ نتيجة الحركة التكتونية للصفيحة العربية، ويحتوي على أحافير (مُستحاثات).

K is for khanjar   خنجر

The khanjar was originally used in the neighboring country of Oman for hunting, skinning animals, and cutting rope. Its blade is made from gold, silver, copper, or brass, and it is now mainly used for ceremonial and decorative purposes.

كان الخنجر يُستخدم في الأصل في سلطنة عُمان المجاورة، وذلك للصيد وسلخ الحيوانات وقطع الحبال. يُصنَع نصله من الذهب أو الفضة أو النحاس أو النحاس الأصفر، ويُستخدم الآن على نحو رئيس للأغراض الاحتفالية والتزيينية.

L is for lizard سحلية

Arabian spiny-tailed lizards are native to the deserts and arid regions of the Arabian Peninsula and other parts of the Middle East. They are known for their distinctive spiny tails, which they use for protection from predators.

موطن السحالي العربية شوكية الذيل الصحراوات والمناطق القاحلة في شبه الجزيرة العربية وأجزاء أخرى من الشرق الأوسط، وهي معروفة بذيولها الشوكية المميزة التي تستخدمها لحماية نفسها من الحيوانات المفترسة.

M is for mosque مسجد

A mosque is a place of worship for Muslims, where they gather to pray and engage in religious activities. It is also a community center that offers resources such as social services, education, and charitable activities. Mosques have architectural features that reflect Islamic beliefs and practices and are considered a sacred space that promotes spiritual reflection and social harmony.

المسجد مكان العبادة لدى المسلمين حيث يجتمعون للصلاة وممارسة الأنشطة الدينية، وهو أيضًا مركز مجتمعي يقدم موارد مثل الخدمات الاجتماعية والتعليم والأنشطة الخيرية. تتميز المساجد بسمات معمارية تعكس المعتقدات والممارسات الإسلامية، وتُعَد أماكن مُقدَّسة تعزِّز التفكير الروحي والوئام الاجتماعي.

N is for najm

نجم

Najm means "star" in Arabic. The North Star shines brightly in the night sky, illuminating the oasis.

كلمة "Najm" تعني "نجم" في اللغة العربية. يسطع "نجم الشمال" في سماء الليل، فيضيء الواحة.

O is for oasis واحة

An oasis is a fertile area in an arid region, sustained by fresh water from underground sources like springs or aquifers.

الواحة منطقة خصبة في وسط منطقة قاحلة تحافظ على استمراريتها بفضل المياه العذبة الآتية من مصادر جوفية، مثل الينابيع أو طبقات تخزين المياه الجوفية.

P is for palm   نخيل

Date palms have been cultivated in the Arabian Peninsula for at least 5,000 years. Dates are an important part of the local economy and are used in traditional dishes. These palm trees are often planted in public places as a way to beautify the landscape and provide shade.

تُزرَع أشجار النخيل في شبه الجزيرة العربية منذ ٥،٠٠٠ سنة على الأقل. تُعَد التمور جزءًا مهمًا من الاقتصاد المحلي، وتُستخدَم في الأطباق التقليدية. وغالبًا ما تُزرع أشجار النخيل في الأماكن العامة لتجميل منظر الأرض وتوفير الظل.

Q is for Al-Qurayyah   شاطئ القرية

Al-Qurayyah Beach is a popular beach near the city of Al Khobar in the Eastern Province of Saudi Arabia. It features a long stretch of sandy beach with clear waters that are ideal for swimming, sunbathing, and water sports.

"القرية" شاطئ شهير بالقرب من مدينة "الخُبر" في المنطقة الشرقية من المملكة العربية السعودية. تتميَّز بشاطئ رملي ممتد طويل مع مياه صافية مثالية للسباحة وحمامات الشمس والرياضات المائية.

R is for Ramadan رمضان

Ramadan is the ninth month of the Islamic calendar and is observed by Muslims worldwide as a month of fasting, prayer, and reflection. During Ramadan, Muslims refrain from eating, drinking, and other physical needs from dawn until sunset. The month of Ramadan is considered a time of spiritual purification and a chance to develop self-discipline, empathy, and generosity.

رمضان هو الشهر التاسع من التقويم الإسلامي، يحتفل به المسلمون في جميع أنحاء العالم بوصفه شهر الصوم والصلاة والتفكُّر. يمتنع المسلمون خلال شهر رمضان عن الأكل والشرب والاحتياجات الجسدية الأخرى من الفجر حتى غروب الشمس. ويُعَد شهر رمضان وقتًا للتطهير الروحي وفرصة لتنمية الانضباط الذاتي والتعاطف والكرم.

S is for shamal   شمال

A shamal is a hot and dry northwesterly wind that can often reach speeds of 20 to 30 miles per hour (32 to 48 km/h) with gusts up to 50 mph (80 km/h), bringing sandstorms and travel disruptions to the Arabian Peninsula. Although shamals can cause damage, they also provide relief from the heat and humidity by bringing dry and arid air from the desert, which can lower the temperature and reduce moisture levels in the atmosphere.

"الشمال" رياح شمالية غربية حارة وجافة قد تصل سرعتها في كثير من الأحيان إلى ٢٠ إلى ٣٠ ميلاً في الساعة (٣٢ إلى ٤٨ كم / ساعة) مع هَبُوب تصل إلى ٥٠ ميلاً في الساعة (٨٠ كم / ساعة) ، مما يؤدي إلى حدوث عواصف رملية واضطرابات في السفر إلى شبه الجزيرة العربية. بالرغم من أن رياح الشمال يمكن أن تسبب أضرارًا، فإنها تخفف من الحرارة والرطوبة عبر جلب الهواء الجاف من الصحراء، مما يمكن أن يخفض درجة الحرارة ويقلل مستويات الرطوبة في الغلاف الجوي.

T is for tent خيمة

Bedouin tents are traditionally used by nomads in the Arabian Peninsula, North Africa, and parts of the Middle East. The tents are made from goat or camel hair and are designed for portability. The hair's natural properties allow it to swell up when it rains, making the tents watertight and resistant to smoke and heat.

يستخدم البدو الرُحَّل الخيامَ البدوية تقليديًا في شبه الجزيرة العربية وشمال إفريقيا وأجزاء من الشرق الأوسط. تُصنَع الخيام من شعر الماعز أو الإبل، وهي مُصمَّمة لتكون قابلة للنقل. الخصائص الطبيعية لذلك الشعر تجعله ينتفخ عند هطول الأمطار، مما يجعل الخيام مانعة لتسرب الماء ومقاوِمة للدخان والحرارة.

U is for Al-Ula علا

Al-Ula is a historic city in northwestern Saudi Arabia that served as a significant crossroads for traders on the incense route. Hegra, also known as Mada'in Saleh, is the main historical site in Al-Ula, featuring well-preserved tombs carved into sandstone cliffs. The tombs are believed to be around 2,000 to 2,500 years old. Today, these popular tourist destinations provide a window into ancient Nabataean architecture and art.

"العُلا" مدينة تاريخية في شمال غرب المملكة العربية السعودية، كانت صلة وصل مهمة للتجَّار على "طريق البخور". موقع "الحِجْر" الأثري، المعروف أيضًا باسم "مدائن صالح"، هو الموقع التاريخي الرئيسي في مدينة "العُلا"، ويضم مقابر محفوظة جيدًا منحوتة ضمن منحدرات من الحجارة الرملية. يُعتقد أن عمر تلك المقابر يتراوح ما بين ٢،٠٠٠ و٢،٥٠٠ سنة. توفر هذه الوجهات السياحية الشهيرة اليوم نافذة على الفن النبطي القديم، ولا سيما فن العمارة.

V is for veil   حجاب

The veil, also known as a hijab, is a traditional headscarf worn by some Muslim women and girls to cover their hair and neck in public. The purpose of wearing a veil is to promote modesty and to preserve the dignity of women. Some Muslim women choose to wear it as a form of religious expression or personal preference.

الحجاب غطاء رأس تقليدي ترتديه بعض النساء والفتيات المسلمات لتغطية شعرهن ورقابهن في الأماكن العامة. الغرض من لبس الحجاب إظهار الاحتشام والحفاظ على كرامة المرأة. تختار بعض النساء المسلمات ارتداءه بوصفه شكلًا من أشكال التعبير الديني أو تفضيلًا شخصيًا.

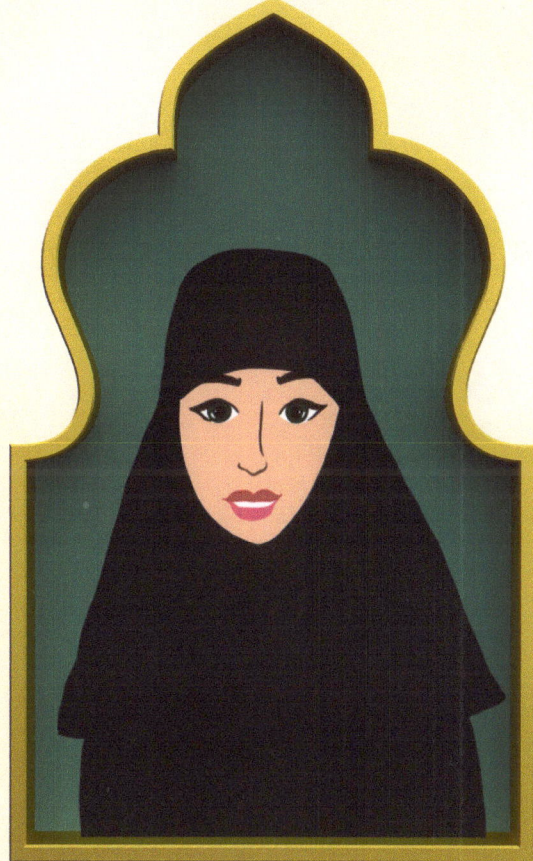

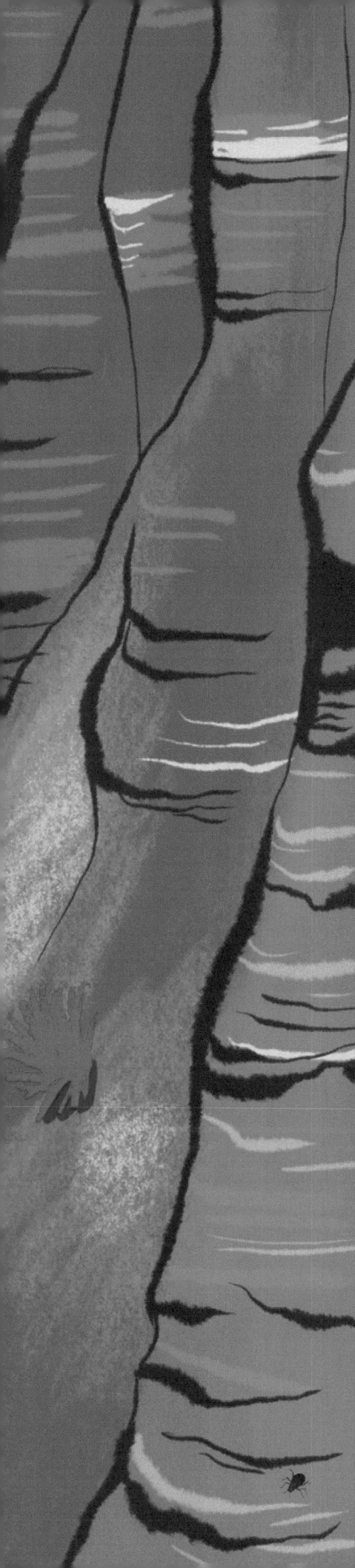

W is for wadi وادي

A wadi is a dry riverbed or valley that only carries water during the rainy season or after heavy rainfall. Wadis are typically found in arid and semi-arid regions of the world and can be dangerous to cross during heavy rains due to flash flooding. Despite being dry most of the time, wadis can be important sources of water and vegetation for plants and animals that live in the desert.

الوادي مجرى نهر جاف أو منخفض أرضي لا يحتوي على ماء إلا خلال موسم الأمطار، أو بعد هطول أمطار غزيرة. توجد الوديان عادة في المناطق القاحلة وشبه القاحلة من العالم، ويمكن أن يكون عبورها خطيرًا أثناء هطول الأمطار الغزيرة بسبب الفيضانات المفاجئة التي تحدث فيها. و بالرغم من أن الوديان جافة في معظم الأوقات، فيمكن أن تكون مصادر مهمة لغذاء النباتات والحيوانات التي تعيش في الصحراء.

X marks the spot تشير العلامة X إلى الموقع

X marks a spot along this journey. Does that tall carved structure look familiar? What is it called? From shark teeth to sand roses, you just might find your treasure in the desert.

تشير العلامة X إلى نقطة أو مكان على طول هذه الرحلة. هل هذا الهيكل الطويل المنحوت يبدو مألوفًا؟ ماذا يُسمّى؟ قد تجد كنزك في الصحراء، بدءًا من أسنان سمك القرش، وصولًا إلى ورود الرمال.

Y is for yalla habibi

يلّا حبيبي

Yalla means "let's go" or "come on," and habibi (for women, habibti) is a term of endearment that means "my dear" or "my beloved." It's a common phrase used among friends and family in Arabic-speaking cultures. In June 2018, the Kingdom of Saudi Arabia allowed women to drive, which was a step towards gender equality and gave them the ability to go places on their own. With excitement, they said, "Yalla habibti, let's go for a drive."

كلمة "يلّا" تعني "هيا بنا" أو "هيا"، وكلمة "حبيبي (للنساء: حبيبتي)" مصطلح تودُّدي يعني "عزيزي (للنساء: عزيزتي)" أو "معشوقي (للنساء: معشوقتي)". وهي عبارة شائعة مُستخدَمة بين الأصدقاء والعائلات في الثقافات الناطق أصحابُها باللغة العربية. في يونيو (حزيران) من عام ٢٠١٨، أصدرت المملكة العربية السعودية قرارًا تاريخيًا سمحت بموجبه للمرأة بقيادة السيارة، فمثّل ذلك خطوة نحو المساواة بين الجنسين، ومكّنَ النساء من الذهاب إلى أي مكان بمفردهن. قالت النساء بحماس: "يلا حبيبتي، فلنخرج في جولة بالسيارة."

Z is for Al-Za'abal Castle

قلعة زعبل

Al-Za'abal Castle is a fortress located near the ancient ruins of the city of Tabuk that was built during the Ottoman Empire in the sixteenth century to protect the pilgrimage route from Egypt to Mecca and Medina. Built using local stone, Za'abal consists of several courtyards and living quarters for soldiers and their families. The fort was restored in the early 2000s and is now open to the public as a museum.

"قلعة زعبل" حصنٌ يقع بالقرب من الآثار القديمة لمدينة "تبوك" المبنيَّة في عهد الإمبراطورية العثمانية في القرن السادس عشر لحماية طريق الحج من مصر إلى مكة المكرمة والمدينة المنورة. القلعة مبنيَّة من الحجارة المحلية، وتتكوَّن من عدة باحات وأماكن سكنية كانت مُخصَّصة للجنود وعائلاتهم. رُمِّمَت القلعة في أوائل العقد الأول من القرن الحادي والعشرين، وهي الآن مفتوحة للعامة بوصفها متحفًا.

In 2020, Athari Alkhaldi was the first Saudi woman to qualify and participate in the Middle East's top falconry competition at the King Abdulaziz Falconry Festival.

في عام ٢٠٢٠، كانت "عذاري الخالدي" أول امرأة سعودية تتأهل إلى مسابقة الصقارة الأبرز في الشرق الأوسط، وتشترك فيها، وذلك في "مهرجان الملك عبد العزيز للصقور".

The desert fox has large ears to hear sounds near and far away, and to stay alert in case of danger. A small body makes it easy to hide. A brownish, pale-red color helps it blend in with the desert. Fur between its toes protects it from the hot sand. Weight: around 2.7 kg (6 lbs)

يمتلك الثعلب الصحراوي أذنين كبيرتين لسماع الأصوات من مسافات قريبة وبعيدة، وللبقاء متيقظًا لأي خطر قد يواجهه. يساعده جسمه صغير الحجم على الاختباء بسهولة، كما يُمكِّنُه لونه البني والأحمر الشاحب من تمويه نفسه في الصحراء. لديه فراء بين أصابع أقدامه يحميه من حر الرمال الساخنة. الوزن: ٢٫٧ كجم (٦ أرطال) تقريبًا.

Most adult lizards grow to about 30 to 40 cm (12 to 15 in). These lizards get water from dew and the food they eat. They have specialized kidneys to conserve water, as well as the ability to store water in their bodies for long periods of time. While these lizards are not dangerous, they can whip their powerful tails and bite when threatened.

تنمو معظم السحالي البالغة لتصل إلى طول يتراوح بين٣٠ و ٤٠ سم (١٢ إلى ١٥ بوصة) تقريبًا. تحصل هذه السحالي على الماء من الندى والطعام الذي تأكله. لديها كلى متخصصة في حفظ الماء، وكذلك القدرة على تخزين الماء في أجسامها لفترات طويلة. رغم أنَّ هذه السحالي ليست خطرة، فإنها تستطيع أن تضرب بذيولها القوية وتعض عندما تكون مُهدَّدة.

Hudhuds boast a large crown of feathers tipped in black and white. Its black-and-white-striped wings have a span of 42 to 46 cm (16.5 to 18 in). The ability to digest poisonous insects makes it immune to many types of toxins. Length: 26 to 28 cm (10 to 11 in). Weight: 47 to 87 g (1.6 to 3 oz)

للهدهد تاج كبير من الريش، مُلوَّن عند أطرافه بالأسود والأبيض. تمتد أجنحته المخططة بالأبيض والأسود على طول يتراوح بين ٤٢ و ٤٦ سم (١٦٫٥ إلى ١٨ بوصة). تعطيه قدرته على هضم الحشرات السامة مناعة ضد أنواع عديدة من السموم. الطول: بين ٢٦ و ٢٨ سم (١٠ إلى ١١ بوصة). الوزن: ٤٧ إلى ٨٧ جم (١٫٦ إلى ٣ أونصة)

Al-Hasa Oasis is a vast and fertile region in Saudi Arabia, with over two million palm trees supporting a thriving agricultural industry. This region is one of the largest producers of dates in the world, with an estimated annual production of over 100,000 tons (90,700,000 kilograms) of dates. This is about the same as the weight of 667 blue whales!

"واحة الأحساء" منطقة شاسعة وخصبة في المملكة العربية السعودية، تضم أكثر من مليوني نخلة تدعم الصناعات الزراعية المزدهرة. تُعَد هذه المنطقة إحدى أكبر المناطق المنتجة للتمور في العالم، إذ يُقدَّر إنتاجها السنوي بأكثر من ١٠٠،٠٠٠ طن (٩٠،٧٠٠،٠٠٠ كجم) من التمور. ويعادل هذا وزن ٦٦٧ حوت أزرق!

Men in the Middle East and North Africa often wear a head cover known as a keffiyeh, shemagh, or ghutra. In Saudi Arabia, the ghutra is typically made of cotton or wool and comes in either an all-white or white-and-red-checkered pattern.

غالبًا ما يرتدي الرجال في الشرق الأوسط وشمال إفريقيا غطاء للرأس يُعرف باسم "الكوفية" أو "الشماغ" أو "الغترة"، ففي المملكة العربية السعودية، تُصنَع الغترة عادة من القطن أو الصوف، وتُصنَع إما باللون الأبيض فقط، أو بالأبيض والأحمر معًا.

Wadi Al-Disah is located in the southwest province of Tabuk in Saudi Arabia. Also known as the Valley of Palms, it is popular for hiking and trekking, camping, rock climbing, swimming, photography, and off-roading.

في الصورة "وادي الديسة"، الذي يقع في جنوب غرب منطقة "تبوك" في المملكة العربية السعودية. يُعرف ذلك الوادي أيضًا باسم "وادي النخيل"، ويشتهر بوصفه مكانًا للمشي لمسافات طويلة، وللرحلات، والتخييم، وتسلُّق الصخور، والسباحة، والتصوير، والقيادة على الطرق الوعرة.

A black Pitted Beetle, which can be found in the desert, has been tracking our journey. How many times did you see our little friend?

تلاحقنا الخنفساء السوداء التي يمكن العثور عليها في الصحراء في رحلتنا. كم مرة رأيت صديقنا الصغير؟

GLOSSARY
قائمة المصطلحات

Ahlan Wa Sahlan _____ أهلًا وسهلًا

Bedouin _____ البدو

Caravan of Camels _____ قافلة الإبل

Dune _____ الكثيب

Empty Quarter _____ الربع الخالي

Falconry _____ الصقارة

Arabian Red Fox _____ الثعلب العربي الأحمر

Gold Souk_____ سوق الذهب

Ghutra _____ الغترة

Hudhud (Hoopoe Bird) _____ الهدهد (طائر الهدهد)

Ithra _____ إثراء

Jebel _____ الجبل

Khanjar _____ الخنجر

Arabian Spiny-Tailed Lizard _____ السحلية العربية شوكية الذيل

Mosque _____ المسجد

Najm (North Star) _____ النجم (نجم الشمال)

Oasis _____ الواحة

Palm Tree _____ شجرة النخيل

Al-Qurayyah Beach _____ شاطئ القرية

Ramadan _____ رمضان

Shamal (Sandstorm) _____ شمال (عاصفة رملية)

Bedouin Tent _____ خيمة بدوية

Al Ula_____ العُلا

Veil _____ الحجاب

Wadi Al Disah _____ وادي الديسة

Yalla Habibi _____ يلا حبيبي

Al-Za'abal Castle _____ قلعة زعبل

ALISON HONG NGUYEN LIHALAKHA lived in Saudi Arabia for six years, where she was known as Ms. Alison to the students at Dhahran Hills Elementary. The library was her favorite place on campus. *ABCs of Arabia* is Alison's celebration of her years in North Africa and the Middle East.

JUSTINE BRAGUY, originally from France, is a colorful illustrator, plant scientist, and dancer currently blooming in the desert of Saudi Arabia. She illustrated the educational coloring book *Under the Red Sea*. Working on *ABCs of Arabia* allowed her to discover and share the gems of the region she calls home.

KHAOULA MAHOUACHI, originally from Tunisia, works at the African Development Bank. In her free time, she enjoys reading in Arabic, English and French.

Published by Kahana Press, Honolulu, HI
www.kahanapress.com

Illustrator: Justine Braguy
Translator: Khaoula Mahouachi
Editor: Pikko's House
Logo designer: Ninja Designers

ISBN (paperback): 979-8-9853226-2-0
ISBN (ebook): 979-8-9853226-3-7
ISBN (hardcover): 979-8-9853226-4-4

Library of Congress Control Number: 2023919413

www.ingramcontent.com/pod-product-compliance
Lightning Source LLC
Chambersburg PA
CBHW061142030426
42335CB00002B/72